Pioneers

JOHN MUIR

rourke biographies

Pioneers

JOHN MUIR

by
CYNTHIA E. LEDBETTER
RICHARD C. JONES

Rourke Publications, Inc.
Vero Beach, Florida 32964

∞ The paper used in this book conforms to the American
National Standard for Permanence of Paper for Printed
Library Materials, Z39.48-1984.

Library of Congress Cataloging-in-Publication Data
Ledbetter, Cynthia Ellen, 1950-
    John Muir / written by Cynthia E. Ledbetter and Richard
C. Jones.
        p.   cm.   — (Rourke biographies. Pioneers)
    Includes bibliographical references and index.
    Summary: A biography of the naturalist who founded the
Sierra Club and was instrumental in early conservation
efforts.
    ISBN 0-86625-494-3 (alk. paper)
    1. Muir, John, 1838-1914—Juvenile literature. 2. Natu-
ralists—United States—Biography—Juvenile literature.
3. Conservationists—United States—Biography—Juvenile
literature.   [1. Muir, John, 1838-1914.   2. Naturalists.   3.
Conservationists.]   I. Jones, Richard C. 1949- . II. Title.
III. Series.
QH31.M9L43   1993
333.7'2'092—dc20
[B]   92-46763
                                                   CIP
                                                    AC

Contents

Color Illustrations

Pioneers

JOHN MUIR

Chapter 1

The Pioneer Spirit

To be a pioneer is to be the first, or one of the first, to do something. John Muir was an environmental pioneer. He was the first to speak out for the protection of American natural areas. Largely self-taught, he became an expert in botany and geology. Muir was an excellent observer of nature and the first to recognize the work of glaciers upon the Yosemite landscape. Although others had wandered the landscape, observing and collecting, Muir was the first to see nature and humankind as interconnected. Today we would recognize him as a *naturalist* or an *ecologist*—a person who studies nature and the interrelationships of its different parts.

A Pioneer's Vision

Muir was different from other naturalists and a true pioneer because he wanted other people to understand his vision. He raised his voice on behalf of nature by sharing his knowledge and love of nature through his writings. After reading Muir's stories, many people became advocates for *preservation*, the protection of nature from destruction and overuse by human beings.

Initially, Muir struggled alone against the forces of destruction so common in the settling of the American frontier. He spoke against wasteful lumbering methods, such as dynamiting trees instead of cutting them. Dynamiting a tree destroys much of its usable lumber, but it is faster than traditional saw cutting, which harvests more board feet of lumber per tree. Overgrazing by livestock, especially sheep, on ecologically fragile grasslands was another of Muir's concerns.

The animals cut the plants to their roots, not leaving enough of the leaf for regrowth. This led to *erosion* (the wearing away) of the soil, which choked the rivers with sediments. Erosion, in turn, damaged the fish population and depleted the soil of nutrients, making the chance of recovery in the next growing season even slimmer.

Farming techniques of that time were also destructive to the soil. Typically, farmers would clear the land of trees and brush, then begin the cycle of planting and harvesting with no thought to fertilization and the effects of erosion. When the soil was exhausted, farmers cut more trees to create more fields, and the cycle continued. Old fields were left to wash into streams or to be slowly reclaimed by weeds.

In addition, the growing human population demanded more water, so new sources had to be found. One quick solution was the flooding of valleys by damming rivers. Muir's campaign to save the Hetch Hetchy river valley in the Sierra mountains of California was one of the first political battles for the environment. The need for water for a growing population was balanced against the protection of a natural area. In this case, the dam builders won. However, this battle continues today, especially in the American west, where water is still scarce.

Muir was one of the earliest environmentalists. He awakened the American public to the value and vulnerability of their natural heritage. In 1892, he and some friends founded the Sierra Club, an organization that would carry on his ideas and fight for the preservation of wilderness long after Muir's personal influence faded. In its one hundredth year, 1992, the Sierra Club was still a champion for the preservation of wilderness areas and wildlife. The questions that Muir raised about the balance between the quality of life and the quantity of life are still with us.

John Muir. (Library of Congress)

Visions of Our World

Muir's vision of how human beings should act and react to the landscape was radically different from that of most other people of his time. Five hundred years ago, when the Europeans came to the New World, they saw a land of seemingly unlimited resources. The new country, as they saw it, was a land to be conquered. Forests were cut to make way for farms. When the soil eroded, the farmers moved to another area, cut down more trees, and started another farm.

By contrast, the peoples of the various Native American tribes viewed the natural world as alive with spirits and considered the earth to be their spiritual mother. They treated the earth and their environment as a partner in life, not as some object to be manipulated. Their attitude is best expressed in the words of the nineteenth-century Columbia Basin chief, Smohalla:

> You ask me to plow the ground! Shall I take a knife and tear my mother's breast? Then when I die she will not take me to her bosom to rest. You ask me to dig for stone [gold]! Shall I dig under her skin for her bones? Then you ask me to cut grass and make hay and sell it, and be rich like white men! But how dare I cut off my mother's hair?

Native Americans believed that spirits reside in all objects and animals; therefore, all living things are holy, a manifestation of God. Their reverence for Earth as the mother of all living things was in direct contrast to the Judeo-Christian belief that human beings rule over nature. It also contrasted with the capitalist ethic of accumulation of wealth.

Muir agreed with the Native Americans and was appalled by the European view that the land and its resources were to be exploited as quickly as possible to turn a profit. Muir wanted to save the wilderness for all people and generations to come. He compared nature to machines that he had designed and built while working in the factories of Indianapolis and

14

Canada. Each part of a machine was significant and contributed to the whole machine's efficiency. Reckless tampering with any one part could destroy the whole machine.

During his lifetime, Muir saw such tampering with nature cause the disappearance of several animal species. First in Scotland, when he was a boy, herring (a type of fish) had disappeared from the market and the dinner tables because of overfishing. Then in America, Muir saw the demise of the bison and the extinction of the carrier pigeon through uncontrolled hunting. He also saw the devastation of many Native American peoples through forced confinement to reservations. Each was a result of the "get rich quick" attitude of European settlers who regarded the land and its peoples as objects to be owned and exploited.

Hickory Hill Farm, near Portage, Wisconsin, where the Muirs settled after immigrating. (John Muir Papers, Holt-Atherton Special Collections. University of the Pacific Libraries, copyright 1984 Muir-Hanna Trust)

A Pioneer's Action

One of the actions that made John Muir a pioneer was that he wrote about his observations and ideas. His first writing was published in the *New York Tribune* on December 5, 1871, and was entitled "Yosemite Glaciers." In this article, he described glaciers as having carved the landscape that created the Yosemite Valley; his writing displayed much of his poetic vision of nature, as well:

> Not a peak, ridge, dome, canyon, lake basin, garden, forest, or stream but in some way explains the past existence and modes of action of flowing, grinding, sculpting, soil-making, scenery-making ice.

Other naturalists of the era had written for academic journals using a dull, descriptive style. Muir wrote about nature by wrapping his descriptions around a story or an exciting narrative. Newspaper editors and readers were more likely to read these exciting accounts than they were to read dry descriptions.

What Made John Muir Different?

Muir lived in a time when the American frontier was being settled—and destroyed. In his youth, he was one of the Europeans who had cleared the land, exhausted the soil, and then moved on to repeat the cycle. By 1890 the United States census had declared the country settled and the frontier gone. Thus, Muir lived during a time when North America was transformed from wilderness to settled farmland. He lived in both of these worlds, and he experienced both the constraints of civilization and the freedom of the wilderness.

Muir watched the wilderness disappear as it bowed to the railroads and other technology of the nineteenth century. He saw ancient Sequoia trees dynamited, rivers dammed, and meadows lost to overgrazing, which in turn led to eroded soil and sediment-choked rivers. Muir believed that there was a better way for people to live, and that was to live in harmony with nature. Native American peoples had no concept of bank accounts and wealth; they believed that all of nature is sacred and should be treated as a gift to human beings. John Muir agreed, and he wanted others to feel the same way.

Chapter 2

Youth

John Muir was born on April 21, 1838, to Daniel and Anne Muir in Dunbar, Scotland. He was the third child of eight and the eldest boy. His father, Daniel Muir, grew up on a farm but later became a merchant in Dunbar, where he worked for more than twenty years. It was there that John and seven of his eight brothers and sisters were born; the youngest would be born later, in Wisconsin.

Because Dunbar lies at the intersection of three ecosystems (an *ecosystem* is a particular "community" of geological and living parts of nature)—the North Sea, the Lammermuir Hills, and the Firth of Forth (the point where the Forth River meets the ocean)—young John had a strong sense of the natural world. Living in a seacoast town gave him an understanding of the sea; at the same time, he could see from his window the folded mountains of the Lammermuirs. John's first eleven years were spent observing the endless but natural struggle between the sea and the mountains.

School Days

As a youngster, John was an active boy with red hair and a keen pair of inquiring eyes. The contrasting geography and weather of Scotland sharpened his powers of observation and taught him how quickly nature could threaten those who were ill prepared. He learned the alphabet before attending school by observing the signs in the shops along the street where he lived.

In school, John studied Latin, French, and English, as well as spelling, history, arithmetic, and geography. His knowledge of French would open a world of literature and travel to him, and the Latin would prove useful in his later studies of botany (the study of plants) and paleontology (the study of fossils).

John's school days were not very happy. The Scottish educational system at this time forced English cultural standards upon its students. Only standard English was spoken in school. Any time Gaelic, Scotland's native language, was spoken, the speaker was reminded with a beating that this was not the language to be used in school. The Scottish method of teaching followed a simple formula: Failure to commit the lessons to memory resulted in another beating.

John also received beatings at home—in punishment for those he got in school, as well as for any failure to memorize Scripture. To a nineteenth-century boy, regular beatings by one's father, teacher, and schoolmates were a normal part of growing up. Popular reasoning of the time favored whipping and beating as methods of building endurance and character— of preparing children for the hardships of life. John recalled a schoolyard game in which two boys would roll up their pant legs, stand toe-to-toe, and hit each other's exposed legs with switches. The first to flinch or make a sound was the loser and fell lower in the schoolyard pecking order.

Perhaps as a result of this treatment, Muir became self-proficient as an adult. He would carry the minimum of equipment and food with him during his journeys and would shun the comforts of life. Indeed, he seemed drawn to hardship and difficult situations. Survival was his victory.

New Beginnings

In 1849, Daniel Muir sold his business and emigrated to the frontier country of America. The great famine of Europe had just ended, and though the Muirs had survived, it was growing more difficult to support a family. Moving to the New World held many attractions for Europeans. Stories of the American

Daniel Muir, John's father. (John Muir Papers, Holt-Atherton Special Collections. University of the Pacific Libraries, copyright 1984 Muir-Hanna Trust)

frontier—often exaggerated and distorted—drifted back to Europe with returning writers, traders, and explorers. The common theme was that the New World was a land of plenty, unlike the famine-ridden Old World. The recently announced discovery of gold in California added to the myth of America as a land of bountiful resources.

Daniel's motive, however, was to seek a life untainted by the hypocrisy and corruption of European churches. John would later describe his father as a Christian zealot who spent his life looking for an uncorrupted church. Daniel thought that America might be the place in which to practice the simple life of a Christian fundamentalist. In America, Daniel followed an evangelical calling, traveling and preaching in the backwoods of the frontier.

At the age of eleven, John and his father, his younger brother David, and his sister Sarah sailed across the Atlantic and settled in Wisconsin. John's mother and his other brothers and sisters did not make the trip at this time, because John's grandfather thought that America was too wild. He insisted that the rest of the family not leave until a proper house and farm had been established. Therefore, they joined the rest of the family a year later. John was excited. He would be released from the routine of school, books, and memorizing.

The Journey

Sailing to the New World was not an easy experience. The forty-seven-day journey was fraught with peril. The Muirs boarded an overcrowded boat with many people suffering what was commonly called "ship's fever" (probably typhus), dysentery, and other diseases that result from overcrowding and unsanitary conditions. The trip was so difficult that many died on the way. Often, the bodies of these travelers were dumped overboard. John's father and Sarah were sick during most of the voyage.

John and David escaped serious illness, however, and enjoyed playing on the deck of the ship. They were free from the beatings at school, and their imaginations were full of stories of the American wilderness. Their ideas about their new home were supported by only a few facts from a book by the American naturalist John James Audubon, *Birds of America*, and by tales from fellow travelers. And then there were stories of California gold.

When the Muirs left Scotland, their destination was Canada. During the voyage, however, John's father heard of the hardships of the Canadian wilderness and that the prairies to the south were better for farming. A religious sect to which Daniel belonged, the Disciples of Christ, had settled in Wisconsin. The stories of the hardships in the north and the thought of friends in the south encouraged the Muirs to shift their destination to the cheap land in Wisconsin.

A New Land

Upon landing in New York City, the family stopped for a few days to recover from the voyage and prepare for the overland journey. John's father arranged passage up the Hudson River to Albany, and then along the Erie Canal to Buffalo. The opening of the canal in 1825 was a major factor in attracting settlers like the Muirs into the Midwest. Along the canal, it was possible to travel by water from New York to Lake Michigan's western shore. However, the flood of people along this route also increased land prices. These high prices drove poorer settlers farther to the West in search of cheaper land.

Arriving in Buffalo, John's father met a member of the Disciples, who gave him information about Wisconsin. The Muirs then took passage on a lake steamer out of Buffalo. It was another crowded voyage. Five days later, they arrived in Milwaukee. From there, a farmer agreed to transport the family and their belongings to Kingstown, about a hundred miles to the northwest.

Kingstown was hardly a town; it was actually a huddle of a few houses and an inn at a crossroads. However, in Kingstown, a fellow Scot helped Daniel choose about eighty acres near the Fox River. The land was blessed with hardwood trees—oak and hickory—and it was bordered by a lake. John's father named the farm Fountain Lake. Native American Indians, members of the Winnebago tribe, lived in tepees across the lake. They frequently visited the farm (mostly to beg), and John was disappointed that they did not wear war paint and carry tomahawks. In his later years, he wrote of them as ragged and dirty; they were not the clean, beautiful, and noble people that the stories of the New World had led him to expect. It was also later in his life that he learned of the treachery and cruelty used against these Native Americans to get their land. The people he remembered across the lake had escaped from the reservation across the Mississippi River to live their final days and die in their homeland near the Fox River. Muir would remember a burial mound near the lake which the Muir family plowed down to grow corn and wheat. As a young boy, however, John did not understand the plight of these people. Nor did he or his family understand the significance of the burial mound.

A New Home

At Fountain Lake, the Muirs lived the life of pioneers, clearing the land and eventually building a house for the rest of the family. They survived the first winter because neighbors helped them construct a log shanty that served as a temporary shelter while a more permanent house was built. The pioneer life was truly a confrontation between human beings and nature. The nearest "neighbor" was about four miles away, and there were no roads between them.

Soon Daniel, John, David, and Sarah were joined by John's mother, his sister Anne, Margaret, Danny, and the twins. John's father later bought 160 acres to the east to expand the farm. Life on the farm was hard, and the amount of work and the harsh living broke the health of all of the children. Although John had escaped beatings from his teachers back in Scotland's schools, he received regular thrashings from his father. A neighbor once commented that "old man Muir works his children like cattle."

As a teenager, John Muir continued to work on the farm. He, his brothers, and his sisters spent most of their days working and their nights reading and memorizing verses from the Bible (the only book of which Daniel approved). Daniel raised John and the other children to appreciate hard work and to respect the strict religion of Scotland, a form of Calvinism. The pioneer life did not leave time for school. In fact, John would attend school for only two months during his teens. Almost all of his skills in reading and writing were learned at the schools he had attended regularly in Scotland.

Lessons from Nature

The "school" that John and his siblings attended in the New World was Nature: Roaming the meadows, climbing trees, caring for animals, and observing the subtle signs of the seasons taught John valuable lessons about life, death, and the relationships of all things to one another.

On the frontier, John witnessed the domestication of the land. Prairies and woods became fields and villages. Animal trails turned into roads and railroads. Settlers continued to arrive. He later recognized this process as the destruction of the land, the exploitation of the Indians, and the work of special business interests to secure for themselves the wealth of the timber, mineral, and water resources. John learned firsthand the injustices perpetrated in the name of progress and

Anne Muir, John's mother. (John Muir Papers, Holt-Atherton Special Collections. University of the Pacific Libraries, copyright 1984 Muir-Hanna Trust)

civilization. This organized aggression disgusted him and drove him further into the wilderness for solitude and a sense of harmony and beauty.

Although he was glad to escape the Scottish schools, life on the farm was no holiday. John rose before sun-up. Fires were not permitted before breakfast, so in the winter he would wake in the cold and have to put his feet into wet socks and then into frozen boots, hoping his body heat would warm them. Chores included feeding horses and cattle, fetching water from the spring, gathering wood, and sharpening tools. Then there was breakfast. Afterward, the heavy work began: chopping trees, building fences, planting and gathering wheat, and performing the hundreds of other tasks necessary to survive on the frontier. John comforted and cheered himself by watching the birds and other animals as he plowed the fields.

Even when they were sick, John and the other children worked the fields, because his stern father believed that hard work and God were all that mattered in this life. Although John referred to their life on the farm as that of "slaves to the vice of over industry," this work was necessary to survive in the wilderness. In fact, many people did not survive. It took the Muirs eight years to build the Fountain Lake farm.

In only eight years, the land was exhausted. Fields that began by supplying twenty-five bushels of wheat per acre now produced only five. The frontier way was one of wasteful extravagance. The country seemed to go on forever; therefore, if the soil lost its productivity or if the trees were burned for fuel, there was always more land just over the hill. This extravagance marked a distinct break from the Old World value of frugality; in the presence of plenty, the European settlers often left that value behind.

In 1856, John's sister Sarah was married, and Daniel Muir sold the young couple the Fountain Lake farm. Cleared land, a house, and fresh water were a good deal for the new couple, even if the land's productivity had fallen. Daniel Muir then bought 320 acres of uncleared land about four miles to the southeast, later naming it Hickory Hill farm. Its beginning in 1857 marked another period of hard labor for John. In fact, he came close to losing his life while digging a well.

Since Hickory Hill farm was not close to a spring, the Muirs needed a well. In a bucket, John was lowered into the hole he dug each morning, brought up for lunch, and then lowered into the hole again to spend the rest of the day digging. John labored many hours each day breaking chunks of rock and dirt, then hoisting them to the top of the well to be hauled away. As the hole got deeper, carbon dioxide built up at the bottom. One morning, after his father had lowered John into the hole, the boy was overcome by the lack of oxygen. It took all of John's strength and willpower to climb back into the bucket before he fainted. He spent many days in bed recuperating from this brush with death. Once he had recovered, however, he was again sent down into the well to finish the work. John wrote later that he resented his father's never working in the well. This incident changed their relationship permanently.

A Budding Inventor

It was at this time that John began to make mechanical devices. As usual, his father did not approve of such activities. In fact, John had to sneak most of his time for reading and tinkering from his grueling workday. In his eleven years at Hickory Hill farm, John's formal schooling amounted to only two months. What education he received, he obtained by trading books with neighbors and teaching himself algebra, geometry, poetry, and literature in the short period between the noon meal and the afternoon shift in the fields, and between 1:00 A.M. and sun-up.

One of John's first inventions was a special alarm clock. This contraption would, at the desired hour, raise the bed and dump the sleeper out onto the floor. Clocks so intrigued John that he stole time from work to perfect his hand-carved wooden clock. He also invented a large mechanical thermometer based on the expansion and contraction of an iron rod. Using a series of levers, he was able to exaggerate the movement of the rod about thirty-two thousand times. With the thermometer set up in the barn, John could read the temperature from across the field he was plowing. This device was such a marvel that his neighbors encouraged him to take it and his clocks to the Wisconsin State Fair, where he might sell his ideas, find a job in a machine shop, or even attend college.

John Muir left the farm after the autumn harvest of 1860. He was both excited and filled with trepidation. On his first train ride to Madison, Wisconsin, he had only one goal: to display one of his inventions at the Wisconsin State Fair. That trip was to be a turning point in his life.

John was the classic country-bumpkin-come-to-town when he arrived in Madison. This aspect of his personality endeared him to the people he met. His booth at the fair attracted many people, and most offered encouragement for his ideas. A natural salesman, John enlisted the help of boys at the fair to demonstrate his inventions. His alarm-clock bed was a real crowd-pleaser.

Several fair-goers suggested that Muir take his inventions to the university across town. He did, and discovered a world with more books than he could ever read, as well as people who were interested in learning about nature. The university was as close to heaven as he had ever come.

Chapter 3

Discoveries

John Muir liked Madison, Wisconsin. There he met Ezra Carr, a professor of natural history, and his wife, Jeanne. They encouraged John to resume his schooling in order to be able to enter the University of Wisconsin in 1861. While John was at the university, two professors were to have a lasting influence on him: James Butler, a professor of classics, and Ezra Carr.

Jeanne was a botanist (she studied plants) and a kindred spirit. She shared John's interest in natural science and introduced him to many friends who shared his interest. She and Ezra knew the eminent poet and philosopher Ralph Waldo Emerson. Jeanne encouraged John to read Emerson's poetry, especially his poem "Woodnotes." She also introduced John to the works of Henry David Thoreau, such as *Walden: Or, Life in the Woods* (1854).

The Carrs and their friends were interested not only in nature but also in the relationship of nature to God and people. Along with Emerson and Thoreau, they were part of a growing movement called Transcendentalism. This philosophy emphasized that nature exists without needing humans to describe it. In other words, humans are only a part of nature; they are not superior to it or necessary for it to continue to exist as the supreme work of God's creation. This philosophy appealed to Muir: Like Native American peoples, he saw nature as having spiritual qualities, not just a material existence.

Hard Times and War

As exciting as it was for the young John Muir to live in

Henry David Thoreau, author of Walden. (Library of Congress)

Madison and attend the university, it was also a difficult time for him. He was desperately poor. His family could not send him any money, so he worked at whatever jobs he could find in order to eat, buy books, and pay his tuition and board. It was also at this time that the Civil War broke out. John visited nearby army camps where some of his friends from his old neighborhood of Fountain Lake were stationed for military duty. John thought that it would be only a matter of time before he, too, would be called. Like others of this time, John did not feel drawn to the issues of the war; he considered himself a Scotsman more than an American. (In fact, it would not be until he was fifty-five years old that he would formally become an American citizen—and then only to get a passport.) Many immigrants felt betrayed by the government, since they viewed the war as a "Yankee" war that had nothing to do with immigrants.

John was horrified by the ravages of war, and at age twenty-five he decided to become a doctor. He thought that he would enter the University of Michigan's medical school in the fall of 1863. However, in the spring of that year, President Lincoln ordered half a million men to be drafted into military service. The Civil War was so unpopular with immigrants that there were riots in Boston which killed 105 people in four days. Of the 292,411 drafted from Wisconsin, more than 52,000 bought their way out of military service by paying a "commutation fee," about 26,000 got substitutes, and more than 40,000 simply did not report. Muir followed his brother, Danny, to Canada.

For Muir, this episode turned into a plant-gathering field trip through Indiana and Michigan and finally into Canada. Muir's love of nature made this field trip last four years. He stopped occasionally to work at factories. In the factories he was able to show the workers and owners how to improve their machinery and methods of production. Muir invented a machine that could make twenty-three thousand broom handles per day; he created other machines that could make rakes. His inventiveness might have led to a successful career in industry, but he felt he was wasting his time.

Jeanne and Ezra Carr. (John Muir Papers, Holt-Atherton Special Collections. University of the Pacific Libraries, copyright 1984 Muir-Hanna Trust)

Sight Lost and Found

Upon his return to Indianapolis, Muir began to attract other nature lovers. Muir would take them on nature walks and tell them stories about his adventures in the Canadian woods. He also supported himself by taking a job in a carriage factory. Muir immediately saw inefficiencies in the manufacture of carriages, so he began inventing machines that would make building the carriages easier.

One day as he was working, he dropped a file on a moving conveyor belt. The file bounced off the belt and flew into his eye. The pain was intense, and Muir believed that he would never see again. As he lay in his darkened room after the accident, he though of how his happiest times had been when he was hiking through the forests and mountains. He was convinced that he would never be able to enjoy the wilderness again. Fortunately, he was wrong: He did recover most of his sight. However, the accident had caused him to rethink his life and his priorities.

Muir decided to devote his life to the study of the natural world. He wanted to be like the German naturalist Alexander von Humboldt and go to the tropics to study the plants and geology of the New World. South America was not the only part of the world that interested him. He wrote to Jeanne Carr asking about a place he remembered reading about: the Yosemite Valley. Yosemite Valley had first been inhabited by Ahwahneechee Indians. They tried to keep white men out, but Major James D. Savage set up a trading post and helped miners establish themselves in this area. The miners actually named the valley; "Yosemite" means "grizzly bear" in the native language.

When he had recovered, Muir returned to Wisconsin. Although the war was over, he said good-bye again to his family and left on a journey that was eventually to take him to California. In September of 1867, Muir took a train to

Louisville, Kentucky, and began what was to become his thousand-mile walk to the Gulf of Mexico. He decided to keep a journal, in which he would write down all of his experiences. To make sure he remembered his minor place in nature, he began his journal with these words: "John Muir, Earth-planet, Universe."

The Thousand-Mile Walk

Muir decided that the best way to get to Florida was to walk. Along the way, he could explore the forests, grasslands, and swamps. As he studied the flora and fauna, Muir kept meticulous notes, which he would later use to write his articles. Any time he ran out of money, he would pause to work at odd jobs. His trip was not easy; sometimes water was so hard to find that he had to drink from mud puddles. The lack of sanitary drinking water, along with Muir's characteristic dislike of spending money, sometimes led to illnesses such as diarrhea and upset stomach. He carried very little with him and did not mind sleeping outdoors in almost any weather. His only fear was that he would be attacked by robbers. In one area notorious for its lawlessness, Muir slept in a graveyard. He spent an undisturbed night, he said, because the highwaymen thought that the cemetery was haunted.

The difficulties of the trip were outweighed, Muir thought, by the opportunities to interact with nature. His understanding of the interdependencies of all parts of nature grew during this trip. He rejected the idea that human beings were the center of God's creation, preferring instead a far wider, more generous view: Human beings, Muir came to believe, were only one among many forms of life, each of which had a special mission to perform. Muir thought that the universe would be just as incomplete if any organism were removed from it as it would be if human beings did not exist. This belief became the most important idea of the environmental movement.

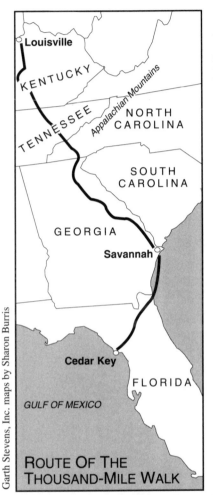

Louisville

KENTUCKY

TENNESSEE

Appalachian Mountains

NORTH CAROLINA

SOUTH CAROLINA

GEORGIA

Savannah

Cedar Key

FLORIDA

GULF OF MEXICO

ROUTE OF THE THOUSAND-MILE WALK

Garth Stevens, Inc. maps by Sharon Burris

As Muir traveled south, he was forced to look for work to support his travels. In Florida he obtained employment at a cedar-log mill. His job did not begin as he expected. Muir came down with malaria. His illness was so severe that he fainted on his way to the mill's bunkhouse. The foreman thought that Muir was drunk and left him lying in the trail for several hours. When Muir regained consciousness, he dragged himself to his bed and collapsed. Several days later he awoke to discover that his employer had taken care of him during his fevered delirium.

When Muir was well enough, he booked passage on a ship to Cuba. Once he arrived, he spent many of his days recuperating from the malaria. In the mornings, he took his lunch and began wandering down the beach. He never failed to see something new and interesting. Many species of plants and animals made their way into his notes. When the sun became too hot and he became tired or hungry, he would rest, eat his lunch, and write in his journal. Then he would begin his walk back up the beach and arrive at his hotel by dinner time. After dinner, he would go to his room and fall asleep.

Each day, Muir followed the same schedule, walking a little farther as his strength increased. Eventually, he made his way into the forests of Cuba, and he wrote in his journal about the hanging vines and beautiful flowers that lived there. Although the plants and animals of Cuba fascinated him, Muir was still anxious to return to New York so that he could book passage on another ship sailing for California and his dreamed-of Yosemite. When a boat arrived that would return to New York, Muir stowed away on it.

At about the same time that Muir arrived in New York, Herman Melville (the author of the famous book *Moby Dick*) was working at the New York waterfront as a customs official. Although Muir wandered the dock area, he and Melville never met. Ironically, Muir also missed an opportunity to visit Central Park, one of the areas of New York that he would have liked. As capable as Muir was of wandering through unmapped forests, he was afraid that he might get lost in the city. Central Park was created by Frederick L. Olmsted, a landscape architect. At that time, Olmsted was chair of the first Yosemite commission; he would eventually succeed in preserving the area as a public park, and Muir would later meet him.

Chapter 4

California

To earn money in order to get to Yosemite, Muir worked as a grain harvester, a wild-horse breaker, a ferryman, and a sheep shearer. By the time he arrived in California, however, he was broke again. Lonely, he wrote to his younger sister Anne:

> I am always a little lonesome Anne, ought I not to be a man by this time & put away childish things[?] I have wandered far enough & seen strange faces enough to feel the whole world a home, & I am a batchelor [Muir's spelling] too. . . . I should not be a boy, but I cannot accustom myself to the coldness of strangers, nor to the shiftings & wanderings of this Arab [Muir meant "wandering"] life.

Muir's wanderings did continue, and although he lived alone, now working as a sheepherder, he could always find interesting things to do. One day he tried to make sourdough bread but found that after it had cooled, it "looked like a cartwheel, and on attempting to cut out a section of it with a butcher knife it broke with a glassy fracture and I began to hope that like Goodyear I had discovered a new article of manufacture."

Wilderness and Wildlife

The mountains around Yosemite, the Sierra Nevada, were alluring. They called Muir to wander their slopes, examining every rock, flower, and animal he spied.

Living the lonely life of a shepherd, Muir had few companions. He did, however, make friends with one of the sheep dogs, Carlos. On many days, while the sheep were grazing, Muir and Carlos would wander through the hills and meadows.

One day, Carlos seemed to become anxious; John followed the dog over a small hill and saw a large brown bear feeding there. Carlos and John snuck down the slope, closer to the bear, and hid behind a tree. The dog was absolutely still and silent, but John peeked out from behind the tree. He was not afraid of the bear; instead, he wanted to study it without scaring it. The bear raised its nose and sniffed the wind, but it continued to stand with its front feet against a fallen tree. John decided that he wanted to see how the bear moved. He had been told that this type of bear was afraid of humans and that any sudden move would send the bear scurrying away.

Confident in his safety, John jumped out from behind the tree, waved his hat in the air, and ran toward the bear, hollering. The bear stood completely erect and lowered its head in a fighting pose. John stopped in mid-stride, surprised and more than a little afraid. He and the bear stood very still and stared at each other for what seemed to John to be a very long time. Finally, the bear slowly turned and lumbered away, looking back over its shoulder occasionally to see if John were following. John wrote in his journal that, although he would have liked to have known the bears of Yosemite better, this land was theirs and he was only a guest.

Mountains and Glaciers

As he hiked through the mountains, Muir tried to imagine the conditions that could have formed the valleys, especially

> *The Sierra Nevada is a mountain range that runs north and south along the "spine" of California and extends approximately four hundred miles. The Muir Trail* (opposite) *extends approximately 218 miles, from Hetch Hetchy to Mt. Whitney.*

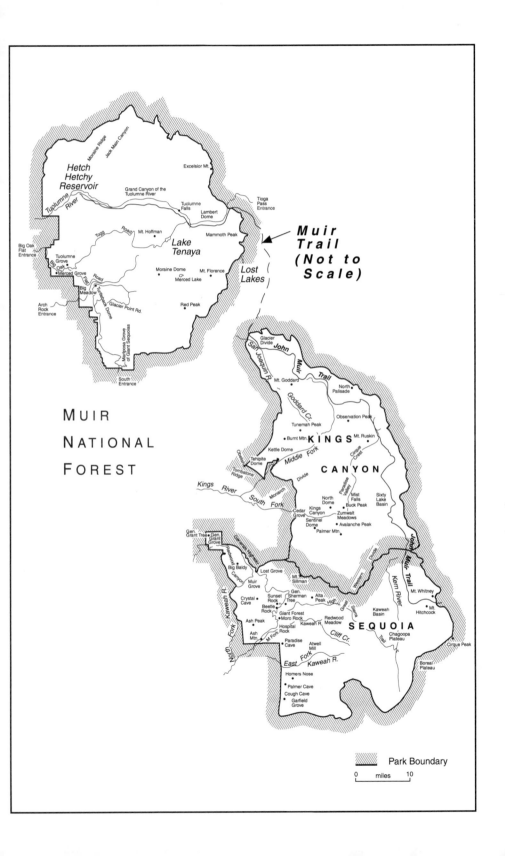

Yosemite. Many geologists of his time believed that some ancient disaster had caused the great scars on the rocks of the mountains and had made great sections of the area sink, creating the valleys. Muir did not think that God had made the world through disasters. He believed instead that natural forces had caused these changes, acting continuously, or uniformly, from the beginning of the world to the present. This idea was known as *uniformitarianism.*

Muir based his ideas on his studies of geology under Ezra Carr and from reading the works of Jean-Louis Agassiz, who had studied European geology extensively. Agassiz's theory was that many mountain valleys were carved from the cliffs by the movement of glaciers. Muir agreed with this *glacial theory* and applied it to the Yosemite area. However, a noted U.S. geologist, Josiah Dwight Whitney, believed that the Yosemite Valley was formed through *subsidence*, a catastrophic event in which the rock layers collapse. Whitney thought that Muir was merely an amateur scientist with little actual knowledge of the Yosemite region or of its geology. Another highly regarded American geologist, Joseph Le Conte, met Muir and spent some time with him hiking through Yosemite. Le Conte felt that Muir had unusually high intelligence and was a good scientist. Still another scientist, and president of the Massachusetts Institute of Technology, George Runkle, also thought Muir's theories were sound. He believed strongly in the glacial theory of the formation of Yosemite and urged Muir to publish his observations.

Muir wanted to be sure his glacial theory was right before he published it, so he was very excited when he found a moving glacier that had left scratches on the sides of the mountains and a path of discarded boulders behind it. One of the first people with whom Muir shared this discovery was his friend and confidante, Jeanne Carr. She encouraged Muir to write articles about his experiences in Yosemite. Finally, Muir

sent an article to the *New York Tribune*. He was very surprised
when the paper actually paid him two hundred dollars. With
this publication came recognition by Agassiz, who stated
firmly that Muir understood glaciers and their effect on the
land.

Muir spent most of the next winter near Yosemite at
Hutchings' sawmill. When he was not working, he conducted
tours of Yosemite Valley. His tours became popular, partly
through the efforts of Jeanne Carr. Ezra had wanted to teach at
the University of California, so the Carrs had moved to
California and occasionally visited with Muir. Jeanne sent
Thérèse Yelverton, a visiting countess, on one of Muir's tours.
Because Hutchings, the owner of the sawmill, had left for the
winter, the rest of Muir's time was devoted to managing the
mill, making sure that Hutchings' wife, Elvira, was
comfortable, and writing letters to Jeanne. His letters told of
his great love for the wilderness and his fear that it would
eventually be consumed by human greed for land and
resources.

In early spring, Muir took a small vacation from the
sawmill. He hiked up into the Sierras and began climbing to
the top of Mount Ritter, which towered over a melting glacier.
Muir got up far enough that he could not turn back. He
realized that he was in danger, so he proceeded with immense
caution. Halfway to the top, he was

> brought to a dead stop, with arms outspread, clinging close to the face
> of the rock, unable to move hand or foot wither up or down. My
> doom appeared fixed. I *must* fall.

Muir closed his eyes and fought his fear. When he opened his
eyes, he found his inner strength and crawled on up to the top.
This ability to find his inner strength was typical of Muir. In
his biography of Muir, *Rediscovering America*, Frederick
Turner states:

Muir would actively, relentlessly seek out adversity and hardship, would relish almost any physical challenge, and would punish himself severely for real or imagined failures to be equal to any circumstance.

Emerson and Other Influences

In 1871, not long after his adventure on Mount Ritter, Jeanne Carr sent Muir a special treat. Ralph Waldo Emerson came to Yosemite to meet Muir. The mountaineer and the philosopher spent several days together at the sawmill but did not go camping, because Emerson's friends thought that, at sixty-eight years of age, he was too frail for that type of activity. Emerson persuaded Muir that he should share his knowledge and love of nature with the public.

Saving the wilderness was a very important goal for many people during this time. Like Muir, people feared that the wilderness might disappear forever if human beings continued to abuse it. Not only did Emerson and Muir share the idea that the wilderness was a vital part of human existence, but others—including naturalists, artists, authors, and educators, such as George Catlin, John James Audubon, George Bird Grinnell, and James Willard Schultz—wrote about humanity's responsibilities to the land.

Emerson's visit was another turning point in Muir's life. He went back to civilization in Oakland, California, and more seriously considered his duties to both nature and his fellow human beings. Muir and Emerson continued to correspond; Muir sent letters and specimens, while Emerson sent two volumes of his collected essays. After Emerson's death in 1882, one of his friends found a list of the men Emerson most admired. John Muir's name was the most recent addition to the list.

For a while Muir lived in Oakland, California, with J. B. McChesney, a high school principal. There he met John Swett, "a pioneer in California public education." They spent long

Ralph Waldo Emerson, leader of the Transcendentalist movement. (Library of Congress)

hours discussing reforms in education and the basic knowledge students should have upon leaving school. Muir had some definite ideas about schooling: "More wild knowledge, less arithmetic and grammar—compulsory education in the form of woodcraft, mountain craft, science at first hand."

Back to Yosemite

Muir spent several months with McChesney while trying to write more articles for publication. However, one evening as

Muir with one of his beloved pines. (John Muir Papers, Holt-Atherton Special Collections. University of the Pacific Libraries, copyright 1984 Muir-Hanna Trust)

he was wandering through the city, he saw goldenrod
blooming. He ran to his room, packed his bag, and fled.

Muir saw civilization as organized insanity. Wheat farming
was wearing out the soil; hydraulic mining was throwing
pollution into streams, which in turn clogged them and caused
flooding; timber was mown down like grass—all because of
greed. Muir felt engulfed, smothered by civilization, trapped
and weighted down. Two nights after he fled, he got his horse,
Brownie, and took off with his friend, A. G. Black, for
Yosemite. That night Muir wrote in his journal that he felt like
a diver coming up for air—exactly as he had felt when he was
pulled from the well on Hickory Hill farm.

Yosemite renewed his spirits and joyously he went hiking
in the Sierras. Muir climbed Mount Shasta and was caught in a
huge snowstorm. He built a shelter and felt quite comfortable
until a search party "rescued" him. As a student of nature,
Muir reveled in experiencing all aspects of it firsthand. Foul
weather was as interesting to him as a tree or a bird, so Muir
was rather irritated with his rescuers, since they kept him from
enjoying the blizzard.

Later, Muir's curiosity prompted him to explore a valley
that led into the Yuba valley. There, he got caught in a
windstorm. Rather than hiding from the storm, he climbed to
the top of a one-hundred-foot Douglas fir tree to smell the
wind and to find out if its source was the mountains or the sea.

As Muir wandered through Yosemite Valley and the
Sierras, he found evidence to support his earlier conclusion
that humans were using up resources at a very fast rate and
were wasting much of those resources. He was afraid that the
majestic Sequoias were seen as massive blocks of lucrative
lumber rather than as a necessary part of nature, and he
worried that the Sierras would be destroyed by timbermen and
sheepherders. Muir knew that the most inaccessible areas were
safe, but these were too few. He once again determined to raise

public awareness of the need to protect these pristine areas. In one of his journals, Muir wrote:

> They will see what I meant in time. There must be places for human beings to satisfy their souls. Food and drink is not all. There is the spiritual. In some it is only a germ, of course, but the germ will grow.

Chapter 5

Alaska

Louie Wanda Strentzel, along with her family, had immigrated to Dallas from England, then moved to California in 1849. Louie and Jeanne Carr became good friends. Jeanne introduced Louie to John Muir in 1872. It took five years for John to begin to show an interest in Louie, but at about forty years of age, he began courting her. Two years later, he proposed to her, and she accepted. Once their engagement was announced, John left for Alaska. Louie was a very understanding person.

During his trip to Alaska, Muir met the Reverend Samuel Hall Young. Although a missionary, Young was also a naturalist and writer. Muir and Young sailed into Thunder Bay to watch a glacier "calve" an iceberg. As they watched, the iceberg majestically began to split from its parent glacier. Young described the fracture as beginning suddenly with "two deep lines of Prussian blue." The fractured portion leaned farther and farther out from the glacier. Finally, Young could contain his excitement no longer. He began jumping up and down, waving his arms and crying, "Hurry up!" With a sound like an explosion, "the great tower of crystal shot up into the air, two hundred feet or more." Muir called this the "largest and most beautiful of bergs."

Treks in the Wilderness

Young and Muir were interested in more than icebergs while they were in Alaska. They also wanted to explore some of the nearby mountains and examine the plants and animals. Muir started up a mountain with Young following after. Young was inexperienced, but he was athletic and thought that he could keep up with Muir. They were to be gone a single day.

Muir told him to watch out for a loose rock, but in his haste to keep up, Young stepped on it and slid down the mountain and over a ledge. At last, he grabbed onto a stable piece of rock and called to Muir for help. Muir came back and carefully worked his way along a sliver of a ledge to get below Young.

Muir and a friend, John Burroughs, in Alaska, 1899. (Library of Congress)

Muir grabbed Young and pulled him onto the ledge. Young's arms were useless, and Muir had to use both his arms and legs to climb, so Muir held Young's collar in his teeth and as Young pushed with his feet, Muir pulled them both to safety. Once safe, Muir set one of Young's shoulders but had to tie the other arm to Young's body. Finally, they made it back to

1. The landscape of Scotland, such as this scene of Loch Etive, helped inspire Muir's love of nature. (Vision Impact Photo Library)

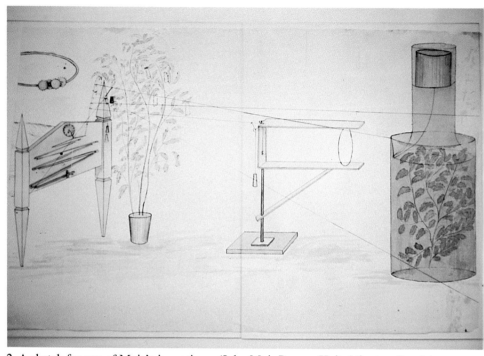

2. A sketch for one of Muir's inventions. (John Muir Papers, Holt-Atherton Special Collections, University of Pacific Libraries, copyright 1984, Muir-Hanna Trust)

3. Muir's California home. (Ben Klaffke)

4. The study in California where Muir did much of his writing. (Ben Klaffke)

5. Muir fought to save ancient trees such as this sequoia at Yosemite National Park. (Lee M. Watson, Unicorn Stock Photos)

6. An artist's interpretation of Muir, on a road leading to Sequoia National Park. (Chris Moose)

7. A cabin to shelter travelers along the John Muir Trail. (Galen Rowell/Mountain Light)

8. The Merced River, Yosemite Valley. (Galen Rowell/Mountain Light)

9. Hetch Hetchy Valley and Reservoir. (Galen Rowell/Mountain Light)

10. Half Dome, Yosemite. (SC Reuman, Visuals Unlimited)

11. Hikers along a trail in Yosemite Valley are framed by a rainbow cast by mist from Vernal Falls. (Galen Rowell/Mountain Light)

12. A hiker pauses along the Muir Trail. (Galen Rowell/Mountain Light)

13. Horseback riders on the Muir Trail, with Banner Peak in the background. (Galen Rowell/
    Mountain Light)

14. The Muir Hut at Muir Pass in Kings Canyon National Park. (Galen Rowell/Mountain Light)

their party, about twelve hours late. The group was angry, but Muir did not defend himself; he went straight to bed. Young was left to tell the tale.

In Alaska, Muir became acquainted with Native Alaskans and with the threat to their culture brought about by "civilizing" them. These people had an understanding of the balance of nature that white people did not. John wrote in his journal that the "good" that Europeans did bring in the form of Christianizing of the Native American peoples caused them to "mope and doze and die on the outskirts of civilization like tamed eagles in barnyard corners." The Native Alaskans were told that they could experience the wonders of nature only through association with the "real" God. Muir felt that Native Alaskan peoples were closer to God than the missionaries who came to preach to them. He noted that the chief of the Stikine tribe, upon hearing that human beings must atone for their sins, offered to give himself as a sacrifice for his people so that God would forgive and bless them. Muir did not see the Indians as savages but as noble people who cared for one another and for their land.

The devastation of California foreshadowed the fate of Alaska ten years after it became a state in 1959. Mountain men helped explore the wilderness, but they wasted the resources. Even with laws to protect the Alaskan wilderness, it is still susceptible to accidents caused by attempts to use its natural resources.

Life at Home

After his travels, Muir came back home to marry Louie in 1880 and settle down. He thought his days of wandering were finished, now that he had a responsibility to his wife and a new family. In 1881, the Muirs' first child, Annie Wanda, was born. Not long after, Louie noticed that John was moping about and that his health had begun to deteriorate. She encouraged him to return to Alaska on the ship *Corwin*. Muir accepted her offer and spent several months exploring a portion of Alaska and enjoying the wilderness, letting his body heal. Later, Louie was able to experience the beauty of Yosemite at first hand when, in 1884, John took her there. He described the sunrise in *Our National Parks*:

> The rose light of dawn, creeping higher among the stars, changes to daffodil yellow; then come the level enthusiastic sunbeams pouring across the feathery ridges, touching pine after pine, spruce and fir, libocedrus and lordly sequoia, searching every recess until they are awakened and warmed.

In one of his letters to daughter Annie Wanda, John added a sketch of himself pushing Louie up a mountain trail. Although Louie was impressed with the beauty and grandeur of Yosemite, she was afraid of bears and mountain lions. She also thought that the lodges, which John saw as luxurious, were primitive. Louie loved her family, the farm, and her garden more than John's wilderness. She did, however, understand his need to be immersed in nature and agreed that he should go on regular trips to re-establish his link with the areas he enjoyed. Louie cherished John's frequent letters during such trips— especially those that contained sketches.

The Muirs' second daughter, Helen, was born in 1886. She was very sickly when she was born; her lungs were weak, and she suffered from breathing problems. John stayed near her side for almost a year. His publishers encouraged him to write while he was at home, but he was too concerned for his daughter's health, so the manuscripts went unattended. John called his daughters his "babies." He took Helen and Annie on nature walks and told them stories of flowers and animals. The girls adored their father and begged him for more stories. He obliged them, and in the process he nurtured their love of nature.

Muir in 1902. (Library of Congress)

The year of Helen's birth was a difficult one for John. It was during this time that he heard that his father was very ill. Although he and his father had differences, John paid for all of his brothers and sisters to go to his father's bedside in Wisconsin. Daniel Muir got to speak with his children one last time before he died.

John's sister Anne was also in poor health. John felt that the Wisconsin winters were too hard on her, so he invited her to move to California. He and Louie welcomed Anne to their home, and she remained there throughout her life.

Louie's father had planted some orchards, which he gave to the Muirs. Muir worked very hard to maintain and improve these groves. He became an excellent farmer and businessman, making an extraordinary living from his crops. Still, Muir was unhappy. He became restless and irritable. One day when Young, whose life he had saved in Alaska, visited him, Muir ran up the road to meet him, asking if Young had come to take him back to Alaska.

Louie knew that the best thing for Muir was to encourage him to go back into the wilderness. She sent him on a camping trip and then wrote him a letter telling him that the only thing that should come before his life in the woods was his children. The Muirs were very wealthy by that time, and the farm was managed by a relative, so Muir was free to travel in the natural environment once again.

Stickeen

Muir eventually returned to visit Young in Alaska, and they set out to explore and measure glaciers. Young was living in Ft. Wrangell with his dog, named Stickeen after the Native American tribe. The little black dog grew quite fond of John, following him everywhere. Muir wrote in one of his journals that Stickeen was a good companion. He even bandaged the dog's paws with his own handkerchief when they became raw from following Muir over the ice.

One day, Young waited in camp while Muir and Stickeen wandered over the Taylor glacier. Muir was, as usual, too interested in his explorations to keep an eye on the weather. A storm blew up, trapping Muir and Stickeen at the edge of a thousand-foot-deep crevasse. Muir used his ax to hack steps down to a bridge. Then he straddled it and slowly slid across to the other side. However, he was still not safe. The far side was straight up, so Muir had to carve more steps into the wall of ice to get out.

When he looked for Stickeen, the dog was whining and running back and forth where John had left him. John called the frightened dog and coaxed him out onto the bridge. Stickeen slowly crawled on his belly across the bridge, then ran up the other side to John. After their joyous reunion, they ran most of the way down the glacier, John shouting and Stickeen barking with excitement. Years afterward, John recounted the actions of his canine companion, calling him a "brave little laddie."

Chapter 6

Parks and Politics

From 1785 to 1886, the U.S. government gave away thousands of acres of public land to individuals and private companies. Muir saw what was happening to the country and fought against it. Yosemite had been declared a state park by Abraham Lincoln, but it was not managed well: Sheep ("hooved locusts," as Muir called them) were destroying pastures of wildflowers. In addition, industry was cutting large sections of trees with no thought as to how this would affect future tree growth or the park in general.

Robert Underwood Johnson, an American diplomat and author, had read some of Muir's writings and shared Muir's feelings about the wilderness. Johnson suggested that a national park be established around the state park. Johnson persuaded Muir to write two articles for the public. Then Johnson would present them to Congress in Washington, D.C., and lobby for a national park. If Yosemite became a national park, federal laws would protect the land and there would be better control of access to the park's more fragile areas.

Muir was very aware of Congress' two arguments against the national park: that the public did not seem to care how public lands were used, and they showed a lack of appreciation for wild lands. John Muir felt, as had Henry David Thoreau, that national parks were necessary to preserve the memory of what forests had once been. Thoreau stated in one of his many writings, "Why should not we who have renounced the king's authority have our own national preserves . . . ?"

Muir's written works regarding Yosemite and a map he drew were the bases of House Bill 12187, which eventually

70

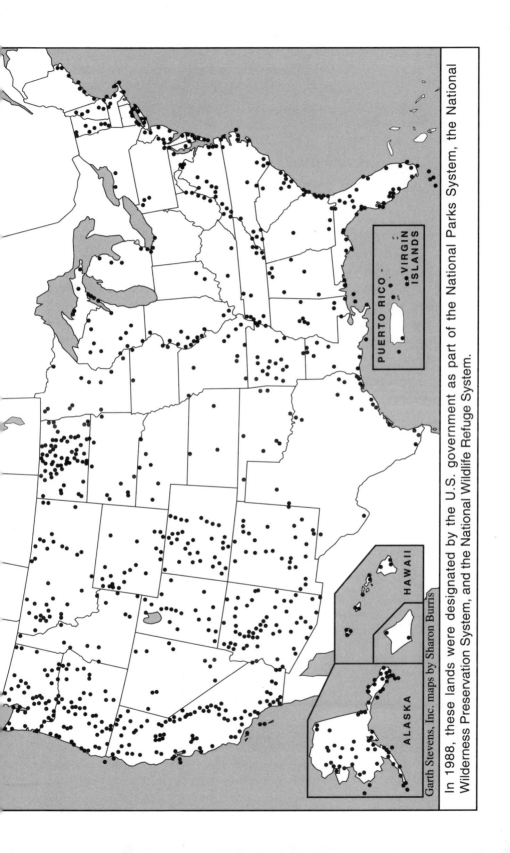

PUERTO RICO -

VIRGIN ISLANDS

ALASKA

HAWAII

Garth Stevens, Inc. maps by Sharon Burris

In 1988, these lands were designated by the U.S. government as part of the National Parks System, the National Wilderness Preservation System, and the National Wildlife Refuge System.

made Yosemite a national park. This was only one of Muir's many successful efforts to use politics to protect nature.

A few years later, Yellowstone—a region of wilderness and hot springs in northwestern Wyoming, southern Montana, and eastern Idaho—was declared a national park but was constantly attacked by commercial interests. Buffalo, which had once roamed the plains in the thousands, had been killed off by white settlers and now numbered only one hundred head, all in Yellowstone. Using his influence again, and with Muir's support, Johnson got the Southern Pacific Railroad, owned by the powerful William Hurst and his family, to become part of a coalition favoring the park. This was an unlikely coalition, because both the railroad and paper industries would have benefited from acquiring land in this area for their own use. The fact that both these industries supported the establishment of the park helped to make Muir's dream a reality.

With renewed public interest in the conservation of the wilderness, Johnson suggested a club for preservation. San Francisco attorney Warren Olney drew up incorporation documents, and Muir gave his support and enthusiasm. In May, 1892, they held the first organizational meeting of the Sierra Club, and on June 4 the articles of incorporation were signed.

Short Trip Home

Wanderlust began to affect Muir again. In 1893, he visited his family home in Dunbar, Scotland. As he walked the streets, he saw many of the friends he had made at school and recognized shops and houses that he had visited as a boy. One of his cousins did not recognize him at first, and when she did, she did not believe her eyes. She asked who he was, and when he told her, she said, "My California Muir!" She welcomed him warmly, and they both greatly enjoyed the visit. Muir noted that two of his old friends still "spoke to him"—the oceans and the mountains remained unchanged.

Muir visited London, Ireland, and Switzerland. He was particularly interested in Switzerland, because it was the country where Jean-Louis Agassiz (the geologist who had developed the glacial theory of valley formation) had been born. Muir visited some of the valleys carved by glaciers and saw that they looked very similar to those in the Sierras.

National Forests

After his return from Europe, Muir was again to become involved in politics. He was asked to visit several states on a fact-finding mission to see how much illegal lumbering was occurring in federal forests. From his research, Muir found that, when the pilgrims had arrived in America in the 1600's, there were more than 400,000 square miles of mature woods on the east coast. By 1800, these woods had been "logged out," along with most of the forests of the Midwest.

During his trip through the states, Muir found that the Black Hills of western South Dakota and northeastern Wyoming had been taken from the Indians and stripped of game and other resources. Indians scarred the land only as much as a beaver or browsing moose. Not so the immigrants, who hacked down everything in their path. Public lands were being wasted and vandalized. Overgrazing and logging caused erosion. Muir wrote that the land could not be stabilized without careful management.

National Parks and Teddy Roosevelt

Soon after his report was published, Muir got a letter from President Theodore Roosevelt saying that he shared Muir's feelings about forest preservation and wanted to talk with him.

Even before he became president, Roosevelt was an outdoorsman and concerned about conservation. In 1887, he

President Teddy Roosevelt (left) with Muir on their trip to Yosemite. (Library of Congress)

went hunting in the Dakotas only to find no elk, no grizzly bears, and only a few wild sheep. The beavers had been trapped out of their ponds, which dried to small streams. The prairie grass had been depleted by cattle and sheep. Roosevelt returned to New York to start the Boone and Crocket Club. He averted the building of a railroad through Yellowstone and pushed the National Park Protective Act of 1894 through Congress. During his presidency, he created fifty-three wildlife preserves, sixteen national monuments, and five new national parks.

In 1903 Roosevelt and Muir went camping in the Sierras. Roosevelt said, "I do not want anyone with me but you, and I want to drop politics absolutely for four days, and just be out in the open with you."

This trip was a high point in Muir's public awareness campaign. He had the full attention of the president of the United States for several days. Such concern for the preservation of nature was rare in American politics, and it would remain so. Muir's association with President Roosevelt reinforced the movement to preserve the wilderness in the form of national monuments, national wilderness areas, national parks, national forests, and wildlife preserves.

Knowing that the president was supporting the preservation of wild areas, Muir felt that he could afford to go traveling again. One of his early dreams had been to see East Asia, Australia, and New Zealand. He began his travels in Europe, then ventured into Russia, and finally reached India and saw the Himalayas. These mountains also showed the work of glaciers, and Muir was pleased that he could recognize evidence of their formation in a region so far removed from Yosemite or Switzerland.

Muir continued his trip by sailing to China, where he had another brush with death. After dining with dignitaries, he contracted ptomaine (pronounced *toemayn*—a severe form of

food poisoning) and almost died. He was carried back onto the
boat on a stretcher and remained in his cabin for several days.
He recovered enough to see Egypt and do some hiking in
Australia and New Zealand.

Now a national figure, Muir returned home and spent most
of 1904 trying to get the portion of Yosemite that was still a
state park back in the hands of the federal government.
Unfortunately, misfortune followed on the heels of Muir's
success.

Muir with wife Louie and their daughters. (John Muir Papers, Holt-Atherton Special
Collections. University of the Pacific Libraries, copyright 1984 Muir-Hanna Trust)

Family Tragedy

Helen was, again, very ill. She suffered from pneumonia, and her lungs were never strong. John took her and Annie Wanda to the Arizona desert in the hope that Helen would soon overcome her sickness. As was her custom, Louie chose to stay home to oversee the farm, tend her garden, and read her books. She did not tell John that she, too, was sick. A few months after they left, John and the girls received word that Louie was, indeed, very sick. They returned to her bedside, but she never recovered.

In 1905, his beloved Louie died, leaving him feeling adrift and lonely. Nevertheless, he tried to remain philosophical about her death:

> This grand show is eternal. It is always sunrise somewhere, the dew is never dried all at once; a shower is forever falling; vapor is ever rising. Eternal sunrise, eternal sunset, eternal dawn and gloaming, on sea and continents and uplands, each in its turn, as the round earth rolls.

At the same time, Helen almost died of pneumonia. Without Louie, Muir had little reason to remain in California. Therefore, he abandoned his notes and returned with Helen to the desert, where her weak lungs could become stronger in the dry climate. Although they took rooms at a hotel, Helen chose to sleep outside, allowing as much fresh air as possible to reach her lungs. Muir wandered in the desert and found as much beauty there as he had found in the Sierras.

The Petrified Forest

It was on one of his walks that John found a forest in the desert. The Chalcedony Park, as it was called at that time, was a forest of fossil trees. John was ecstatic, and he spent quite a lot of time studying the trees with a magnifying glass. The area was being frequented by tourists, however, and manufacturers of abrasives (rough substances used in polishing or cleaning) had tried to remove the petrified trees and grind them up to use in their product. The people living in the area and a paleo-biologist named Lester Ward urged Congress to remove this portion of Arizona from further homesteading in order to protect it.

Of course, John added his voice in support of these efforts. In 1906, Congress passed the Antiquities Act, which protected not only fossils but other features, such as Indian villages, as well. President Roosevelt declared the Chalcedony Park a national monument, and it came to be known as the Petrified Forest. It became a national park in 1962, thanks to John Muir's early interest and his efforts to save the fossil trees.

The desert was not to be Muir's permanent home. When Helen was well, she and her father returned to their home in California so that he could continue his writing. Muir was astounded by the volume of the notes he had accumulated during his life and overwhelmed by the task of shaping these notes into books. Then, the politics of his cause once more demanded Muir's attention. His writings were again left incomplete.

Muir (seated) at the Petrified Forest in Arizona, ca. 1906, with daughters Annie Wanda and Helen on either side. (John Muir Papers, Holt-Atherton Special Collections. University of the Pacific Libraries, copyright 1984 Muir-Hanna Trust)

Chapter 7

End of an Era

One of Muir's greatest accomplishments was the founding of the Sierra Club. He was "hoping to do something for wilderness and make the mountains glad." The mission of the club was, and still is, "to explore, enjoy, and protect the wild places of the Earth."

The Sierra Club

Although the group began with about one hundred people, the Sierra Club has grown to more than three-quarters of a million members. The original members thought of their group as an outing club; however, they began to realize that they could have an impact on the protection of the environment if they also functioned as the "watchdogs of Yosemite." The club managed both these functions fairly well. Shortly after its beginning, Sierra Club members found that they could perform many services to the land and to the people who enjoyed it. For example, they began recording the names of the people who went mountain climbing, keeping track of who was on the mountain and whether these adventurers became lost.

In 1901, however, the club seemed to be floundering. The meetings were taken up with bureaucratic business rather than the business of teaching people about nature and preserving the wilderness. Muir and several of the leaders of the club decided that revitalization was in order. They sponsored a field trip to Yosemite. Muir, his daughters, and about one hundred members of the club camped for more than a month. They spent their time wandering about, studying the plants and animals, and reviving their love of nature in Yosemite Valley and Tuolumne Meadows. Field trips became a tradition in the Sierra Club, and the organization's work for the preservation of wild places continued.

By 1903, the club had grown enough to have an office building in San Francisco. This building not only was the headquarters but also housed the club's collection of books. Unfortunately, the original site was destroyed in the San Francisco earthquake of 1906, along with the club's library and all its records. By 1909, however, the Sierra Club was growing again. Members volunteered their time to build trails in the High Sierra, above Kings Canyon. This began a Sierra Club tradition of keeping the trails of national parks in good condition for hikers.

Hetch Hetchy

Hetch Hetchy was a beautiful river valley at the foot of the Sierras. Politicians saw that the water from the Tuolumne River, which formed this garden spot, was needed by the people of San Francisco. They proposed to dam the river and flood the valley, forming a reservoir for the city. Muir believed that this area, like Yosemite Valley, deserved protection by the federal government. Yosemite Valley and Hetch Hetchy Valley, he wrote, had

> level parklike floors and walls of immense height and grandeur of sculpture. This middle region holds also the greater number of the beautiful glacier lakes and glacier meadows, the greatest granite domes, and the most brilliant and most extensive glacier pavements. And though in large part it is severely rocky and bare, it is still rich in trees.

Muir began to fight with San Francisco for the life of Hetch Hetchy.

Muir did not know it, but his fight was lost before it had begun. The Right of Way Act of 1901 allowed cities and towns to take land they needed for the welfare of their inhabitants. This law, along with the devastation of San Francisco by the fires caused by a massive earthquake in 1906, would eventually doom Hetch Hetchy. However, at the time that Muir began his fight, he was unaware of his future defeat. He spoke

Muir (pointing) gives a tour to members of the Sierra Club, on the trail to Hetch Hetchy. (John Muir Papers, Holt-Atherton Special Collections. University of the Pacific Libraries, copyright 1984 Muir-Hanna Trust)

so angrily and intensely against the damming of the Tuolumne River that he was banned from several environmental groups that had previously supported him and was not invited to their meetings. Some of Muir's opponents accused him of defending Hetch Hetchy and Yosemite out of arrogance and selfishness. Some even accused him of putting the issue ahead of his family. This made Muir sad and caused him to wonder if the beauty of nature was wasted on the general public.

The fight for Hetch Hetchy went on for six years and drained Muir's energy. The federal government refused to protect the area. Muir saw this sacrifice of Hetch Hetchy to the cities and private interests as a betrayal of the national trust, and he was extremely disappointed in President Roosevelt for not rescuing this wilderness area. Permission was given for the flooding of the Hetch Hetchy Valley in 1913. In 1914, the Sierra Club took its last outing to this garden spot. The original dam was built in 1923 and expanded in 1938. The flooding turned the once beautiful valley into a lake nine miles long, which is also used for electrical power generation. Today, for much of the year, the water table is low, due to drought, and Hetch Hetchy Valley is a mud flat, full of rotting tree stumps.

The Final Trek

Intellectually, emotionally, and physically exhausted, John fell back on the activity that had always healed his body and spirit. He returned to the wilderness. In his youth, Muir had been inspired by the writings of the German geographer Alexander von Humboldt. Muir had dreamed of traveling to South America, as Humboldt had done. In the summer of 1911, at the age of seventy-three, John Muir finally got to "play Humboldt" and visit the forests of South America.

Once the fight was lost and emotions dropped to normal levels, Muir was eventually accepted back into the environmental groups from which he had been excluded. Now he was in demand for interviews. The members of these groups regarded Muir as more knowledgeable about nature than possibly anyone in the nation.

In the winter of 1914, Muir caught the grippe (a form of
influenza), but he insisted on continuing work on his writings.
Helen had married and moved to the Nevada desert. She had
had one child and now gave birth to a second baby. Because it
was close to Christmas, Muir decided to visit his new
grandchild. During his stay in the desert he began to feel
somewhat better; however, this did not last. The doctor was
called and diagnosed Muir as having double pneumonia. He
was taken to a hospital in Los Angeles, where again he seemed
to rally.

People visited him regularly; Muir told them that he was
feeling better but that he was tired. The nurses asked the
visitors to leave so that Muir could rest. According to
Frederick Turner, one of Muir's biographers, "At the end there
was no great wrestling against the fading of the light, but
rather a simple sauntering into the next season"—as though
Muir were headed out on another one of his hikes. Muir
himself best summed up his life:

> I only went out for a walk, and finally concluded to stay out till
> sundown, for going out, I found, was really going in.

John Muir died on Christmas Eve, 1914.

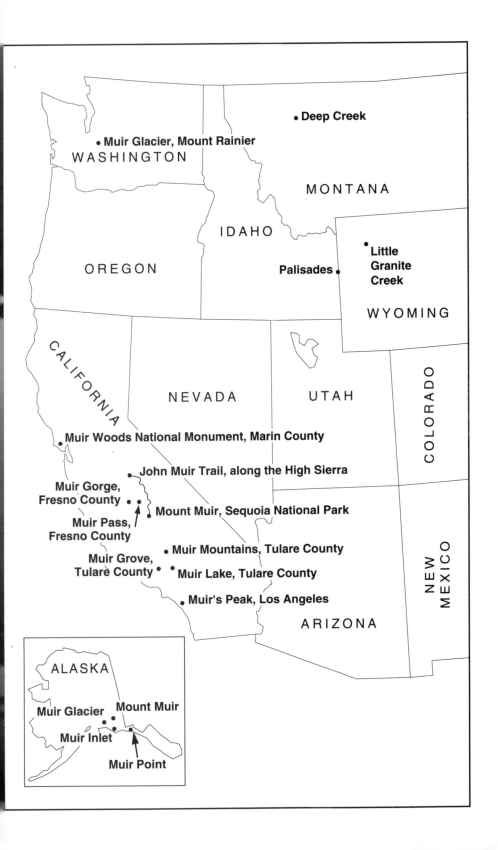

Deep Creek

Muir Glacier, Mount Rainier
WASHINGTON

MONTANA

IDAHO

OREGON

Palisades

Little
Granite
Creek

WYOMING

CALIFORNIA

NEVADA

UTAH

COLORADO

Muir Woods National Monument, Marin County

John Muir Trail, along the High Sierra

Muir Gorge,
Fresno County

Mount Muir, Sequoia National Park

Muir Pass,
Fresno County

Muir Mountains, Tulare County

Muir Grove,
Tulare County

Muir Lake, Tulare County

Muir's Peak, Los Angeles

ARIZONA

NEW
MEXICO

ALASKA

Muir Glacier   Mount Muir

Muir Inlet

Muir Point

Chapter 8

Muir's Legacy

John Muir's influence upon the American environmental movement did not die with him. When Muir died, the manuscript for *Travels in Alaska* was at his bedside. Two friends finished typing his notes and wrote an introduction for the work; it was published in 1915. In the years since his death, Muir's writings have been republished and incorporated into many other works.

A Wilderness to Cherish

What John Muir accomplished is still with us. His idea of preserving the wilderness so that it could be studied and enjoyed is seen in today's national park system. His influence was especially strong in the preservation of the Yosemite Valley, Yellowstone, the Grand Canyon, Mount Rainier, and the Petrified Forest. In fact, his work was so important that today he is considered to be "the father of our national parks." Many areas have been named after Muir to honor the man and his accomplishments. One example is the John Muir Trail, which winds approximately 218 miles through three national forests and three national parks. This beautiful path begins near Hetch Hetchy at the Tuolumne meadows in Yosemite National Park and ends at the foot of Mount Whitney in Sequoia National Park. Each year millions of people experience nature through visits to these parks.

Parks have perhaps become too popular. The sheer volume of people passing through has caused damage to some areas. In Yosemite, cars are banned from some areas and there is a limit to the number of people who can visit at any one time. Even

Muir ca. 1912. (Library of Congress)

with limitations and restrictions, the air pollution and erosion that visitors inflict on the park are challenging its ability to recover. It would be ironic if Muir's struggle to educate people about natural areas, to appreciate and learn from nature, were the very source of their destruction. As people enjoy the national parks, it is important for them to remember that these are fragile areas: leaving behind even a small bit of trash or toxic waste can irreversibly damage the plants and animals.

Today's Sierra Club

Although many once viewed the Sierra Club as simply a group of naturalists who went camping together, it has become much more than that. Once the "watchdog of Yosemite," the club has become a "watchdog of the environment." This role began with the industrialists and railroad magnates who wanted to build railroads; the Sierra Club urged Congress to establish the National Park Service in 1912. Since then, the club has been in the thick of many political battles for the land.

Over a period of twenty years, from 1939 to 1959, the Sierra Club played a vital part in blocking the construction of six dams that would have flooded three national parks.

The Sierra Club's involvement in environmental protection was evident again in 1961, when it opposed and made public Project Chariot. Industrialists had interests in the resources available in Alaska, but the area in which they wanted to dock their boats was too shallow. They wanted the government to allow them to set off a nuclear explosion to dredge out a harbor. Once the public heard of this plan, they let Congress know of their displeasure, and the project was scrapped.

In 1964, the Sierra Club was instrumental in the passage of the Wilderness Act—the first set of laws in the world to protect the environment. Not long after these laws were passed, the government wanted to dam the Colorado River and flood the Grand Canyon. The Sierra Club was quick to bring this plan to the attention of the American public by taking out full-page advertisements in newspapers. The government responded by supporting the Internal Revenue Service, which states that contributions to the Sierra Club were no longer tax-deductible. That year saw the biggest increase in dues-paying members in the club.

Other successful actions sponsored by the Sierra Club are many: stopping the pollution of Lake Superior; banning DDT (a poison that affects birds and animals as well as insects); using highway funds to support mass transit; establishing several wilderness areas, such as the Alaskan national parks; eliminating the crosscutting of trees on federal lands; strengthening the Clean Air Act; recalling Secretary of the Interior James Watt (who wanted to reduce the size of many national parks and prohibit the formation of new national parks); banning MX missile tests; and establishing U.S. policy to protect the Antarctic environment.

The Sierra Club has also established its Legal Defense Fund. The club's lawyers represent anyone, from neighborhood groups to entire Native American nations, who is interested in protecting an area from destruction. In their first case, they saved California's Mineral King Valley from becoming a ski resort. This small valley is on the edge of the Sequoia National Park. Walt Disney wanted to cut down trees and build highways, motels, trams, and restaurants to bring thousands of tourists into the area. The Sierra Club showed that such changes would destroy the area's wildlife. Eventually, Mineral King Valley was made a part of the national park.

Lawyers from the Legal Defense Fund believe that their clients are not simply people but also plants, animals, and land. Admiralty Island in Alaska, killer whales, owls, dolphins, sea lions, and whales all fall under their protection. The lawyers believe that the generations who follow are also their clients.

To do their jobs, they must remind Congress that there are laws protecting the environment and that those laws must be enforced.

There is now a permanent branch of the Sierra Club in Washington, D.C. The members at this branch keep up with events—such as plans to dam rivers—that could threaten the wilderness. Had such a branch existed in Muir's time, Hetch Hetchy might never have been flooded.

Today's Environmental Movement

The preservation movement has grown, and those who have followed in Muir's footsteps have continued to gain significant political power. Today, the preservation movement is alive and well: We know it as the environmental movement. Groups such as the Sierra Club, the Wilderness Society, Defenders of Wildlife, and The Nature Conservancy educate and organize people for the preservation of natural areas. Colleges and universities teach courses in ecology and offer majors in environmental studies and technology. These courses teach students how all parts of the natural world interconnect and affect each other, and how best to use our natural inheritance without wasting or destroying it. That is exactly what Muir was writing about more than one hundred years ago.

Muir's legacy is also the struggle to teach people that they are part of—not apart from—nature. Many people believe that human beings are entitled to use as much of Earth's resources as they want and that future generations can worry about themselves. Those who have studied Muir's philosophy believe that human beings are *not* the most important part of the world but, rather, that all of nature—in fact, Earth itself—must be our highest priority if we and our children are to survive beyond a few more generations. As Muir saw when he invented machines, Nature, the most wonderful machine, is not here as our servant; we are simply part of the machinery.

Some of the events that have taken place since Muir's death make this view obvious: In Muir's time, thousands of cars and factories did not pour poisonous gases into the air; today there are many cities where children's lungs are weakened by the time they are in middle school, and smog is even rising into Muir's beloved Sierras. In Muir's time, chemicals were not widely used to kill pests, increase crop production, or artificially boost the growth of plants and animals; today, these substances have begun to work their way into our bodies in the food we eat and the water we drink. In Muir's day, there was no nuclear energy; today, testing of nuclear weapons and the use of nuclear energy plants have threatened us with radiation poisoning—but, at the same time, this technology, if safely controlled, promises to help eliminate our use of the carbon-based fuels (such as gasoline) that have ruined the air. Muir's vision is even more amazing, then, when we realize that he lived in a much cleaner world and was still able to foresee some the problems we face today.

Even within environmental groups, there is disagreement about the stewardship of the earth. On one side, those who might be called "conservationists" battle those who might be called "preservationists," on the other side. *Conservationists* try to balance our human activities of development and profit with the need to protect the environment. *Preservationists* value the protection of nature above all other goals. Muir would probably side with the preservationists. It is through Muir's legacy that many people today understand the fragile interrelationships that drive our planet's ecology. Our quality of life and our general health are dependent upon how well we take care of the earth's systems.

The challenge for us is to make difficult decisions about the quality of life for ourselves and future generations. Our exploding population is at the heart of our environmental problems. Simply, the more people there are, the more resources are consumed. More trees are cut down; more land is mined for minerals and fuel; more engines burn fuel to run cars, trucks, and factories, which in turn pollute the air, water, and earth. People need the basics of food, water, clothing, and shelter. All these come from the earth. How may we extract resources at faster and faster rates without harming the earth's ability to continue to produce them for future generations? Who gets to use all these resources? Should they be shared evenly or should the rich nations get to have as much as they want?

Seeing Green

John Muir left the parks for people he would never see or know. But his legacy goes beyond the beauty of the physical spaces; it also lies in the understanding we derive from those areas. His goal was for us to understand and respect the interconnectedness of our lives with the earth. We must develop this understanding and pass it on to the generations who come after us.

In the late 1960's and early 1970's, the astronauts who traveled to the Moon during Apollo space missions took the first pictures of Earth. One of these photographs captures the entire globe on a single photographic frame. This image reminds us that Earth is a very special yet fragile place. Images from other space missions, such as those returned to Earth from the Voyager space probes and the Hubble Space Telescope, remind us that there is only one place like Earth. As big as Earth is, it is not infinite. Our consumption of limited resources, garbage disposal, and pollution control are posing problems for all Earth's people. Our portrait from space reminds us that we are all in this together. There is no such thing as pollution or garbage going away—there is no "away," only "here."

The pictures of Earth that our spacecraft have returned to us

Always looking forward. (Library of Congress)

reveal that our world is even more remarkable than Muir could have imagined. Yet, had Muir lived long enough to see the pictures of Earth from space, it is doubtful that they would have expanded his vision very much. He probably would have said, "I knew it all along."

Organizations

The following organizations work to protect the environment. The addresses are for the national headquarters, but local chapters may exist in your community or a nearby city.

Canadian Parks and Wilderness
    Society
Suite 1335, 160 Bloor Street East
Toronto, Ontario
Canada M4W 1B9

Conservation International
    Foundation
1015 18th Street NW
Washington, DC 20036

Council on Environmental Quality
722 Jackson Place NW
Washington, DC 20503

Defenders of Wildlife
1244 19th Street NW
Washington, DC 20036

Environmental Defense Fund
257 Park Avenue South
New York, NY 10010

Environmental Protection Agency
401 M Street SW
Washington, DC 20460

Greenpeace, Inc.
1436 U Street NW
Washington, DC 20009

National Audubon Society
700 Broadway
New York, NY 10003

National Park Service
Department of the Interior
P.O. Box 37127
Washington, DC 20013-7127

National Wildlife Federation
1400 16th Street NW
Washington, DC 20036

Natural Resources Defense Council
40 W. 20th Street
New York, NY 10011

The Nature Conservancy
1815 Lynn Street
Arlington, VA 22209

Population Reference Bureau
1875 Connecticut Avenue NW
Suite 520
Washington, DC 20009-5278

Resources for the Future
1616 P Street NW
Washington, DC 20036

Sierra Club
730 Polk Street
San Francisco, CA 94109

United Nations Environment
    Program
New York Liaison Office
2 United Nations Plaza

Room 803
New York, NY 10017

Wilderness Society
900 17th Street NW
Washington DC 20006

World Environment Center, Inc.
419 Park Avenue South
Suite 1800
New York, NY 10016

World Wildlife Fund
1250 24th Street NW
Washington, D.C. 20037

Worldwatch Institute
1776 Massachusetts Avenue NW
Washington, DC 20036

Yosemite Association
P.O. Box 545
Yosemite National Park, CA 95389

Time Line

1838   John Muir is born to Daniel and Anne in Dunbar, Scotland, on April 21.

1844   Samuel F. B. Morse demonstrates long-distance communication between Baltimore and Washington, D.C., with the telegraph.

1845   Europe's potato crop failure triggers famine in Europe. *The Condition of the Working Class* (a portrait of conditions in working-class Europe), by Friedrich Engels, is published.

1847   Asa Gray's *Manual of Botany* lists all the known plants in the northern United States.

1848   Gold is discovered in California, encouraging a wave of immigration and prospecting.

1849   The Muir family emigrates to America, settling at Fountain Lake farm, Wisconsin.

1857   The Muir family moves to Hickory Hill farm, Wisconsin.

1859   Edwin Drake drills the world's first oil well in Titusville, Pennsylvania. Charles Darwin publishes *On the Origin of Species.*

1860   John Muir leaves home for the Wisconsin State Fair in Madison; he meets Jeanne and Ezra Carr. Abraham Lincoln is elected president of the United States.

1861   New York and San Francisco are connected by telegraph. The Civil War begins.

1862   Muir's second year at the University of Wisconsin in Madison; he teaches elementary school for part of the year. The great Transcendentalist philosopher and author of *Walden*, Henry David Thoreau, dies. Congress passes the Homestead Act, which gives land to people who settle the frontier.

1864   Muir leaves Wisconsin for Canada. He spends time exploring and takes a job in a sawmill near Meaford, Ontario, with his brother, Daniel.

1866   Muir returns to America after the Civil War, settling in Indianapolis. He works for a carriage factory, where he develops labor-saving procedures. The Great Leonid Meteor Shower also occurs in this year.

1867   In March, Muir is temporarily blinded in a factory accident. As his vision returns, he decides to abandon factory work and study nature. In September, he begins his "thousand-mile walk" to the Gulf of Mexico. Also in this year, George Westinghouse solves a major railroad problem with the invention of the air brake. Railroads flourish across the country.

1868   Muir visits Cuba, New York, and California. At age thirty, he sees Yosemite for the first time.

1869   Working for Pat Delaney as a sheepherder, Muir develops a glacial theory for the formation of the mountains and valleys of Yosemite. The Atlantic and Pacific coasts are connected by rail; settlers now have access to the entire country.

1870   Muir spends the winter in Yosemite Valley and works at Hutchings sawmill. In the spring he begins giving tours of Yosemite. The Carrs move to California.

1871   Muir publishes "Yosemite Glaciers" in the *New York Tribune*. Ralph Waldo Emerson visits Muir at Yosemite. Also in this year, a great slaughter of passenger pigeons occurs in Wisconsin.

1872   Muir begins his writing for the magazine *Overland Monthly*. Yellowstone National Park is established.

1875   Muir moves to San Francisco and writes for the next five years. He protests the lumbering of California's giant Sequoias.

1876   Muir writes *God's First Temples*, in which he explains the interconnections of nature and how human beings should strive to protect its fragile balance; this book makes his the first voice in the preservation debate. Also in this year, Alexander Graham Bell invents the telephone and the Centennial Exposition showcases technology that has helped tame the American frontier.

1877   Muir travels in Utah and California. He continues writing and lecturing.

1879   Muir becomes engaged to Louie Strentzel. He leaves on his first Alaskan expedition. Also in this year, Thomas Edison and Joseph Swan invent the electric light bulb.

1880   Muir marries Strentzel on April 14.

1881   The Muirs' first daughter, Annie Wanda, is born. Because of Muir's poor health, Louie encourages him to go to Alaska aboard the ship *Corwin*.

1882 Ralph Waldo Emerson, the leader of the American Transcendentalist movement, dies.

1884 Muir takes Louie to Yosemite.

1885 Muir's father, Daniel, dies.

1886 The Muirs' second daughter, Helen, is born.

1887 Muir begins work on his book *Picturesque California*.

1888 Muir is outraged by damage done at Mount Shasta and Mount Rainier. *Picturesque California* is published. The National Geographic Society is founded. George Eastman introduces the first commercial roll film camera, making photography available to the public.

1889 Muir meets Robert Underwood Johnson, who persuades Muir to write articles to protect Yosemite.

1890 Muir completes two articles for the magazine *Century*. This heralds his return to public life. The Yosemite and Sequoia national parks are established. Also in this year, more than two hundred Sioux Indians are massacred by U.S. troops at Wounded Knee, South Dakota, a "battle" that marks the final conquest of the North American Indian by European settlers. The U.S. census announces the disappearance of the American frontier.

1892 The Sierra Club is formed.

1893 Muir returns to Scotland and Europe. Upon his return to the United States, he meets many literary and scientific people in New York.

1894 *Mountains of California* is published.

1896 Muir's mother, Anne, dies. Muir joins the U.S. Forestry Commission.

1897 Muir publishes "Forest Reservations and National Parks" in *Harper's Weekly* and "The American Forest" in *The Atlantic Monthly*. Both articles create popular support for preserving national forests.

1898 Muir lobbies for preservation in Washington, D.C.

1899 Muir travels to Alaska. Mount Rainier National Park is established.

1901 President William McKinley is assassinated, and Vice President Theodore Roosevelt becomes president. Muir begins correspondence with Roosevelt about natural resources. *Our National Parks* is published.

PIONEERS

1902   Richard Bosh invents the spark plug, making the internal combustion engine (and therefore gasoline-powered automobiles) possible.

1903   Muir and Roosevelt camp in Yosemite. The Wright brothers fly the first successful airplane at Kitty Hawk, North Carolina.

1904   Work begins on the Panama Canal. John Fleming invents the vacuum tube, paving the way for radio.

1905   Louie Muir, John's wife, dies.

1906   Reginald A. Fessenden invents AM radio.

1908   Muir Woods National Monument and Grand Canyon National Monument are created.

1909   *Stickeen* is published.

1910   Charles Proteus Steinmetz, in *Future of Electricity*, warns about air and water pollution.

1911   Muir publishes *My First Summer in the Sierra*. He sets sail for South America and Africa.

1912   *The Yosemite* and *Edward Henry Harriman* are published.

1913   Muir publishes *The Story of My Boyhood and Youth*. The first home refrigerator goes on sale in Chicago. Henry Ford introduces the assembly line and begins mass-production of automobiles.

1914   John Muir dies in Los Angeles on December 24. Traffic lights are introduced to regulate the flow of cars. World War I begins on July 28 with the assassination of Austrian Archduke Francis Ferdinand.

1915   *Travels in Alaska* and *Letters to a Friend* are published.

1916   The National Park Service is established to protect and manage land. *A Thousand-Mile Walk to the Gulf* is published. John Fisher develops the modern washing machine.

1918   *Steep Trails* is published.

1920   The first regular licensed radio broadcast occurs.

1938   *John of the Mountains: The Unpublished Journals of John Muir*, edited by Linnie Marsh Wolfe, is published.

1949   *Studies in the Sierra* is published.

Glossary

Botany: A branch of biology that focuses on the study of plants.

Botanist: A person who studies the biology of plants.

Conservation: The careful use of resources so that they will sustain human activities.

Conservationist: A person who advocates the wise and conservative use of Earth's resources. *See also* **Preservationist.**

Ecology: The study of interrelationships between living things and their environment.

Ecologist: A person who studies the interrelationships of the various parts of nature.

Ecosystem: a particular "community" of geological and living parts of nature.

Environment: A general term describing Earth's life forms and the geographies in which they live.

Environmentalist: A person who is concerned about the wise use of Earth's resources and the quality of life for its people.

Erosion: The carrying away of rock or soil by wind or water.

Fauna: A scientific name for all animals.

Flora: A scientific name for all plants.

Geology: The study of the history of the earth, often by observing and analyzing rocks and land formations.

Glaciation: The evidence of glaciers upon the surface of the land. Muir postulated that glaciers created the landform of Yosemite.

Glacier: A vast, slowly moving body of ice that acts like a bulldozer, gouging the surface of the earth as it moves across land.

Moraine: A mound or hill formed by the bulldozer action of a glacier.

National monument: An area protected by the government to preserve an interesting natural feature or historic site.

National park: An area of scenic or ecological value protected by the government for people to enjoy and study. National parks are usually larger than national monuments.

Naturalist: A person who studies nature. Generally applied to a scientist who works in the field rather than in a laboratory. *See also* **Ecologist.**

Preservation: The protection of a species or area from destruction.

Preservationist: A person who wants to protect rather than use natural resources. *See also* **Conservationist.**

Sequoia: A large variety of redwood tree which grows in northern and
central California. There are two varieties: *Sequoia sempervirens,* which
are the trees that are in the Muir Woods, and the *Sequoiadendron
giganteum,* a huge variety, thousands of years old.
Sierra: A Spanish word meaning "saw." The early Spanish explorers gave
this name to the Pacific coast mountains, which had a jagged profile that
resembled the teeth of a saw.
Sierra Nevada: In Spanish, this means "snow-covered saw." A range of
mountains extending north and south along the eastern part of California.
Uniformitarianism: A theory in geology that assumes that the processes
that have shaped the earth in the past are essentially the same as those
acting today.
Wilderness: An area protected from development or resource exploitation
by human beings.

Bibliography

Books and Writings by John Muir

John Muir: Mountaineering Essays. Edited by Richard F. Fleck. Salt Lake: Peregrine Smith, 1984. A collection of Muir's notes and writings during the "western" chapter of his life. Much of the focus is on the Sierras and Alaska. Muir's style helped persuade Congress to establish the park service.

John Muir: To Yosemite and Beyond, Writings from the Years 1863 to 1875. Edited by Robert Engberg and Donald Wesling. Madison: University of Wisconsin Press, 1980. Selected essays by Muir, showing his philosophy about nature.

John of the Mountains: The Unpublished Journals of John Muir. Edited by Linnie Marsh Wolfe. Boston: Houghton Mifflin, 1938. Puts Muir's unpublished works in chronological order and fills in some of the gaps.

Letters to a Friend. Boston: Houghton Mifflin, 1915. A collection of letters to Jeanne Carr, a botanist who became Muir's dearest friend. Muir describes his travels and his feelings about nature.

The Life and Letters of John Muir. 2 vols. Edited by William F. Bade. Boston: Houghton Mifflin, 1923. An annotated collection of Muir's letters. Many of these letters were edited by Muir himself. A primary source for his written work.

The Mountains of California. New York: Century, 1894. Examines the formation of the Sierras and the area's abundant wildlife.

My First Summer in the Sierra. Boston: Houghton Mifflin, 1911. Recounts Muir's first impressions of the Sierras.

Our National Parks. Boston: Houghton Mifflin, 1901. Explains the geology and botany of Yosemite and Yellowstone.

Picturesque California. San Francisco: J. Dewing, 1888. Short essays, edited by Muir, which describe areas of Yosemite, the Sequoias, and the Sierras. Muir is the editor.

Steep Trails. Boston: Houghton Mifflin, 1918. Notes, published after Muir's death, about the preservation of wilderness areas.

Stickeen. Boston: Houghton Mifflin, 1909. The story of one of Muir's trips to Alaska. Muir describes his experiences with a loyal and brave dog.

The Story of My Boyhood and Youth. Boston: Houghton Mifflin, 1913. Recounts Muir's life prior to his leaving home for the University of Wisconsin.

Studies in the Sierra. San Francisco: Sierra Club, 1949. Explains the formation of the Sierra mountains and valleys.

A Thousand-Mile Walk to the Gulf. Boston: Houghton Mifflin, 1916. Describes Muir's experiences during his travels to Cuba.

Travels in Alaska. Boston: Houghton Mifflin, 1915. Unfinished works about Muir's experiences in Alaska.

The Wilderness World of John Muir. Edited by Edwin Way Teal. Boston: Houghton Mifflin, 1954. A collection of Muir's notes and notebooks kept during his various journeys. A primary source for his writings.

The Yosemite. New York: Doubleday, 1912. A detailed description of the formation of Yosemite Valley, including its flora and fauna. Muir also relates the struggle to gain national park status for the area.

Books About John Muir

Buske, Frank, ed. *Wilderness Essays.* Salt Lake City: Peregrine Smith Books, 1980. A collection of some of Muir's best-known works. Muir's writing is clear and direct, demonstrating his keen powers of observation in figures of speech, similes, and metaphors from the natural world.

Clark, Margaret Goff. *John Muir, Friend of Nature.* Champaign, Ill.: Garland, 1974. A book for the younger reader. This work portrays the life of Muir in a historical account of the highlights of his life. A good introduction to John Muir and his philosophy of conservation.

Cohen, Michael. *The Pathless Way: John Muir and the American Wilderness.* Madison: University of Wisconsin Press, 1984. Muir's philosophy and the plight of the wilderness are explored. Muir asks European Americans to value the philosophy of the Native American peoples they are destroying.

Douglas, William O. *Muir of the Mountains.* Boston: Houghton Mifflin, 1961. This tale of real-life adventure is well written for the younger reader.

Fleck, Richard F. *Henry Thoreau and John Muir Among the Indians.* Hamden, Conn.: Archon Books, 1985. Muir spent much time with Native Americans of several tribes and referred to them often in his writings. In this collection of his "Indian notebooks," it is clear how their philosophy influenced Muir. Native Americans confirmed Muir's belief in the need for a harmonious relationship with nature and made him more aware of the interdependence of nature and human beings.

Fox, Stephen. *John Muir and His Legacy: The American Conservation Movement.* Boston: Little, Brown, 1981. A readable biography of the man and the history of the movement to save the natural environment. This work goes beyond Muir to include other Americans who have contributed to the conservation movement.

Leopold, Aldo. *A Sand County Almanac*. New York: Oxford University Press, 1949. Leopold was Muir's voice in the generation of environmentalists after Muir died. Many ideas here are a testament to what was becoming, in the 1940's, Muir's legacy. Very readable.

Lyon, Thomas. *John Muir*. New York: Twayne Publishers, 1965. The voice of a pioneer is recognized in the era of revitalized environmental awareness. A very readable work that emphasizes the integrated philosophy Muir developed as a result of his life experiences with nature.

Norman, Charles. *John Muir: Father of Our National Parks*. London: Julian Messner, 1957. An account of Muir's struggle to acquire federal protection for wilderness areas.

Tolan, Sally. *John Muir: Naturalist, Writer, and Guardian of the North American Wilderness*. Milwaukee: Garth Stevens, 1989. A well-written and well-illustrated account of the life and philosophy of John Muir. One of the better selections for the middle school student.

Turner, Frederick. *Rediscovering America: John Muir in His Time and Ours*. New York: Viking Penguin, 1985. This work organizes Muir's life into four main sections. Not only describes events of his time but also speaks to ours in the context of other Yosemites.

Wadsworth, Ginger. *John Muir, Wilderness Protector*. Minneapolis: Lerner, 1992. This book sheds light on Muir's home life. The author writes about Louie and Muir's daughters extensively. She also deals with how Louie supported Muir's philosophy.

Wolfe, Linnie Marsh. *Son of the Wilderness: The Life of John Muir*. Madison: University of Wisconsin Press, 1943. This very readable work explores Muir as a person. The multifaceted man championed many unpopular causes, and some people sought to destroy his influence. This work explores the credibility of the many myths and stories surrounding John Muir.

Young, Samuel Hall. *Alaska Days with John Muir*. New York: Fleming Revell, 1915. Recounts Young's adventures with Muir. Many of the passages parallel those written in Muir's journals. Descriptions of the flora, fauna, and geology of Alaska are included.

Media Resources

America: Domestication of a Wilderness. Video, 52 minutes. 1989. Distributed by Ambrose Video Publishing, Suite 1601, 381 Park Avenue South, New York, N.Y. 10016. One of a series hosted by Alistair Cooke. In this segment, he examines the settlement of the West by the European immigrants in the fashion that the Muirs settled in Wisconsin. Further emphasis is given to the development of the transcontinental railway and the struggle of Native Americans to preserve what was left of their culture and lands.

The Garden of Eden. Video, 28 minutes. 1987. Distributed by Direct Cinema Limited, P.O. Box 69589, Los Angeles, Calif. 90069. This work addresses the question of extinction and how rare species have been used to develop new antibiotics, disease-resistant corn, and improved insect repellents. One message of this program is that extinction is permanent and it is our duty to leave our descendants a wide variety of life.

Guide to Yosemite National Park. Video, 52 minutes. 1991. Distributed by VCRI, P.O. Box 11779, Gillette, Wyo. 82717. Yosemite was one of John Muir's favorites places. This video tours the twelve hundred square miles of Yosemite, revealing it as a land of granite monoliths carved by glacial forces, geological erosion, and sedimentation. The giant Sequoias are also shown.

John Muir: Father of Our National Parks. 16mm film, 15 minutes. 1973. Distributed by Disney Educational Services, Burbank, Calif. Part of the "They Made a Difference" series, this film presents the life and inner conflicts of Muir, beginning with his boyhood and continuing through the naturalist, inventor, lecturer, author, and adviser to presidents.

John Muir: The Man, the Poet, the Legacy. Video, 50 minutes. 1992. Distributed by Bridgestone Publishing Group, 1991 Village Park Way, Suite 180, Encinitas, Calif. 90060. Shows the geology and geography of the Sierras. Gives examples of Muir's journal writing.

John Muir's High Sierra. Video, 27 minutes. 1974. Distributed by Pyramid Films, 1888 Century Park East, Suite 1000, Los Angeles, Calif. 90067. A biography of Muir, tracing his responsibility for the creation of Yosemite National Park and the formation of the Sierra Club.

Powerful Medicine. Video, 44 minutes. 1988. Distributed by Film Incorporated, 5547 North Ravenswood, Chicago, Ill. 60640-1199. About half of modern drugs are based on the chemical factories of plants. Many thousands of plants remain unexamined for their medical benefits. The extinction of about five hundred plants per year poses a loss of invaluable medicinal benefits. This video examines the race to discover and protect the benefits of valuable species.

Race to Save the Planet. Series of nine hour-long videos. 1987. Distributed by Intellimation, P.O. Box 1922, Santa Barbara, Calif. 93116-1922. A compelling look at how people are changing the face of the planet. The episodes are entitled "The Environmental Revolution," "Only One Atmosphere," "Do We Really Want to Live This Way?," "In the Name of Progress," "Remnants of Eden," "More for Less," "Save the Earth . . . Feed the World," "It Needs Political Decision," and "Now or Never." Together, these programs present a global perspective on the declining health of the planet. The series also asks viewers to join in the search for workable solutions to the crisis.

Water Wars. Three videos, 49 minutes each. Produced by the British Broadcasting Corporation, 1992. Distributed by Films Incorporated Videos, 5547 N. Ravenswood Ave., Chicago, Ill. 60640. The episode "Good as Gold" focuses on the water problems of the American West, made famous by Muir's Hetch Hetchy campaign. "To the Last Drop" explores the politics of water in Russia's neighboring nations. In all three videos, the series underscores the point that to have water is to have power. To be without water provokes political and social turmoil.

What Are We Leaving for Our Children? Video, 75 minutes. 1989. Distributed by The Windstar Foundation, 10 Park Avenue, Suite 300, Basalt, Colo. 81621. The fourth annual Windstar Symposium in 1989 asked this question. Jeremy Rifkin speaks on global environmental security and the greenhouse crisis.

What You Can Do to Save the Planet. Video, 30 minutes. 1990. Distributed by Intellimation, P.O. Box 1922, Santa Barbara, Calif. 93116-1922. After identifying the ills of modern life in an ecological context, this video describes some practical and easy ways to slow the environmental degradation of the planet.

Pioneers

JOHN MUIR

INDEX